"GIVE 'EM HELL HARRY"

Samuel Gallu

"GIVE 'EM HELL HARRY"

Reminiscences

The Viking Press   New York

First published in 1975 by The Viking Press, Inc.
625 Madison Avenue, New York, N.Y. 10022
Published simultaneously in Canada by
The Macmillan Company of Canada Limited

LIBRARY OF CONGRESS CATALOGING IN PUBLICATION DATA
Gallu, Samuel.
    "Give 'em hell Harry."

    1. Truman, Harry S., Pres. U. S., 1884–1972—Drama.
I. Title.
PS3557.A416G5   812'.5'4   75–22388
ISBN 0–670–34165–7

Printed in U.S.A.

ACKNOWLEDGMENT

Oliver Berliner and Associates: *Congratulations, Tom Dewey.*
Words and music by Richard M. Sherman & Milton P. Larsen.
(From the record album "Smash Flops," produced by Oliver Berliner.)
Copyright © 1959 by Hall of Fame Music Co.;
assigned to Annandale Music Co. All rights reserved.

*The photographs and cartoons used are reproduced
with the kind permission of the following:*

Associated Press: pp. 75, 77
Thomas A. Engelhardt and the St. Louis *Post-Dispatch*: p. 31
International News Service: pp. 16, 58–59
Kansas City *Star*: pp. 11, 36 *(bottom)*
Bradley Smith: p. 83
Harry S. Truman Library: pp. 7 (photo by Bachrach), 21 *(top)*,
    25, 29, 36 *(top)*, 55 (U. S. Army Signal Corps photo)
United Press-International: pp. 38, 46, 53, 63, 65, 79
U.S. Army Signal Corps: p. 33
U.S. Navy: p. 21 *(bottom)*
Wide World Photos: p. 3

For
MARGARET TRUMAN DANIEL
With Appreciation

"GIVE 'EM HELL HARRY"
by Samuel Gallu

Presented as a play with

> Harry S. Truman, Alvanley Johnson, A.F. Whitney,
> Charles Ross, Tom Clark, Herbert Hoover, Eddie
> Jacobson, Dr. Wallace Graham, Dr. Chevalier
> Jackson, Franklin Delano Roosevelt, Sue Gentry, Bess
> Truman, Tom Pendergast, Margaret Truman, Paul
> Hume, Louise Hackmeister, Rose Conway, Sam
> Rayburn, General George C. Marshall, General
> Douglas MacArthur, Richard Nixon, the American
> people, and members of the Press.

Produced by Samuel Gallu and Thomas J. McErlane
The role of President Truman played by James Whitmore
Directed by Peter H. Hunt
Scenic Designer James Hamilton

First performance, Community Theatre, Hershey, Pennsylvania,
March 19, 1975

Gala Premiere, Ford's Theatre, Washington, D.C., April 17, 1975

> Hosts: Margaret Truman Daniel and Secretary of the
> Interior Rogers C. B. Morton

> In attendance: the President of the United States
> Gerald R. Ford and Mrs. Ford; members of the
> Cabinet, the Congress, Diplomatic Corps, and other
> dignitaries.

The author gratefully acknowledges the cooperation received from members of the Truman family, friends, colleagues, relatives, and associates of the late President Harry S. Truman; also from the Harry S. Truman Library in Independence, Missouri, for information, documents, audio-visual aids, and hitherto unrevealed materials and recollections.

"GIVE 'EM HELL HARRY"

The stage is dark. The lights come up revealing President Truman at his White House desk. The set is a duplicate of the one in the Truman Library. It looks sketchy and impressionistic, not like a full, permanent set. Stage right is a desk like the ones used by senators in the U.S. Senate. Leaning against the set, stage left, is a lawn mower—a plain old-fashioned push mower. On President Truman's desk is a sign that reads: "The Buck Stops Here." President Truman is very nattily dressed in a double-breasted suit, white shirt, and white handkerchief, well starched and prominently displayed from his breast pocket. On his left wrist he wears a chronometer-type watch.

He is in the midst of writing a letter.

• • • And so, Margaret, to be a good President, I fear a man cannot be his own mentor. He cannot live the Sermon on the Mount. He must be a Machiavelli, Caesar, Borgia, an unctuous religio, a liar, a what-not, to be successful. So I probably won't be, thanks be to God. But I'm having a lot of fun trying the opposite approach. Maybe it will win. Lots of love, Dad. . . .

He folds the letter, puts it into an envelope, and takes a three-cent stamp from his wallet which he licks and places on the face of the letter. Then he flips the intercom switch.

1

Say, Rose, are Mr. Johnston and Mr. Whitney there yet? They are. All right, now what about the attorney general? Good, Tom Clark's here. And Charlie Ross? Fine, send them all in.

The men are Alvanley Johnston, head of the Brotherhood of Locomotive Engineers, A.F. Whitney, president of the Brotherhood of Railroad Trainmen, Charlie Ross, press secretary, and Tom Clark, attorney general of the United States.

Good morning, gentlemen. Good morning, nice to see you, Mr. Johnston, Mr. Whitney, Charlie, Tom. Well, gentlemen, what have you worked out on the proposed settlement? You mean to tell me that eighteen of your twenty railroad brotherhoods are willing to accept the arbitration award, but you're going to stop the railroads from running anyhow? Well, boys, if I knew you were going to tell me that, I wouldn't have asked you over here this morning. God may have built the earth in six days, but that was certainly before labor unions. You think I'm going to sit here and let you tie this whole country up, you're crazier than hell. You've got forty-eight hours to reach a settlement. If you don't, I'm going to take the railroads over in the name of the government. That's all, boys . . . I said, that's all.

He holds up his hands as though to hold off the remarks of the other men.

President Truman with representatives of the railroad unions

2

Oh, I know. I know, Charlie. Charlie, listen, I know just as well as you do that their union's always backed me politically, but this is not a case of labor versus management. This is a case of a few big money boys in management and the war rich unions against the government, and I'm going to teach them to exercise some social responsibility. I'm trying to get this country back on a peacetime footing, and I'm not going to have the private citizen getting the hind tit on this deal. It's got to be fair all around. I'm going to take the hide of those bastards. This damn inflation business has got to stop, and that goes for the National Association of Manufacturers crowd as well. They're not going to stampede me into lifting price controls. You think we ought to consult some economists, do you, Charlie? Well, let me tell you I dropped into a few supermarkets on my walk the other day, and I don't need those economic wizards to tell that this country is hurting. All you got to do is see how it's buying. The only thing that's going to stop this thing is a few swift kicks in the right asses. Besides, if you laid those economists end to end, they'd point in all directions. No, sir, if we leave this to management, why, prices would go so high you'd wish you were in the undertaking business just to pick up the newly dead. They'd show you net profits, rather net greed, that would have every labor leader in this country screaming for higher wages. And then they'd both be yelling that I was interfering with private enterprise. No, sir! If we leave it to management and labor, why, people won't be able to buy any more, and of course that's what management wants. Then they'd yell "sales lag," lay off a lot of workers, and the unions would get panicky. They'd tone down their demands, ask for

4

less money, which is exactly the way management planned it all along, and then of course, they'd give the working fellow just enough to get him buying again—on the installment plan, I might add. They say they're for competition, well, they're for eliminating competition. I'm sick of this government being viled and flouted and the people bankrupt and ruined. I may have inherited this job, but, by God, I'm in charge and they damn well better know it! That's all, boys.

> *The two men get up and leave.*
> *Truman watches them. He thinks about what's been said and then picks up a copy of the* Washington Post *and scans it.*

There's only one way to deal with the tough issues— *head on and the hell with the consequences.*

> *He gets up from his desk and walks down stage center.*

I never saw myself as President. I was just in the right place at the wrong time. Lots of folks could do a better job, but it became mine to do, and as long as you put me here, you'll get the best I've got. I've always thought of myself as an ordinary man. I don't have any special personal endowments, and I don't waste time worrying about what I don't have. I just try to do the best with what I do have. I've always felt it's not important how you do something or say it, the point is to get it said and done. I don't waste time comparing myself to other men—no reason to. I don't compare myself to Roosevelt or Winston Churchill. All men do things differently. I'll tell you what I mean now. . . . One time I ran into the all-time great American snob, the Lady Astor. I'm sure you've heard of her. Well, she's a transplanted Virginian and she developed such a strong British accent that even the British couldn't understand her —let alone stand her. I ran into *the Lady* at some ceremony down in Williamsburg. She made some rather unkind remarks about my Missoura accent. Well, I cut her short by saying that at least my accent was honest. Now Winston Churchill, on the other hand, does things a little differently. He ran into the Lady at a dinner party in London. It was the kind of dinner party that Winston truly enjoys, and he derives most of his joy out of imbibing in rather large amounts of brandy. *The* Lady was seated next to him and she undertook to give the Prime Minister a lecture. She said, "Mr. Prime Minister, I believe you are quite drunk." Winston looked at her and said, "You're quite right, my Lady, I am quite drunk. And my Lady, you are unbelievably ugly, but tomorrow morning I will be indisputably sober.". . .

Referring to the newspaper:

Well, Herbert Hoover's in town. You know the one trouble with this job is that when you leave it, you got to find something else to do. Really, it's hell for a man to try to find work once he's been President of the United States.

A family portrait

6

He picks up the phone.

Hackie, get me the Shoreham Hotel, would you please? No, no, just put it through and I'll handle it. Thank you.

To the audience, as he waits:

You know, he's quite a man, Herbert Hoover. He did a great job after World War I, feeding all those poor unfortunates in Europe. We rewarded him with this job, and of course the Depression hit and we all turned on him. The Depression was not created by Herbert Hoover, it was created for him. Most of us forget that he instituted the Reconstruction Finance Corporation, which was to keep the small businesses going when the commercial banks turned their backs on them. Banks, boy, there's a bunch of crooks for you. They're happy to lend you money when you prove you don't need it. You want a friend in life, get a dog!

Into the phone:

Shoreham Hotel, yes, would you connect me with Herbert Hoover, please. Harry Truman . . . That's right, Harry Truman, 1600 Pennsylvania Avenue. Well, all right . . . oh, fine . . . well, it was nice chatting with you, too.

Connection is made.

Mr. President, Harry Truman . . . how . . . oh, all right. Mr. Hoover, this is the President. Yes, say, I'd like to come up to see you. . . . I thought you might feel that way. That's all right if you want to come down here, fine. I'll send a car for you. . . . Not at all. Look forward to seeing you.

He flashes for Hackie on the phone.

Hackie, would you send a car to the Shoreham Hotel immediately and pick up Mr. Herbert Hoover. Let me know the minute he arrives.

To the audience as he rises, walks around the desk, and moves center stage.

Of course, one thing in favor of this job is that when you get it, you move into a nicely furnished and rather comfortable house. It wasn't always that way. When John Adams and his Abigail moved into this place, it was just a great big unfurnished barn that had no heat, no furniture. Abigail, in fact, had to hang her laundry in the East Room. The President that tried to complete it and furnish it somewhat was Thomas Jefferson. Jefferson built the north and south porticos and the elaborate terraces out there. Those terraces were originally built to hide the hen houses. They tell me that the best looking, the best dressed, and the highest living fella that ever held this office was Chester Arthur. They say he even looked like a President. He kept a whore on the premises. Now back home, we call a fella like that "a widower with means." Since I've had the office,

9

I've always hoped that I'd run into Lincoln's ghost, but I never have. They say Teddy Roosevelt talked to the famous man all the time. I think that being a Republican must have helped.

Phone rings.

Yep, all right, put it through. Hello, Eddie, how the hell are you? . . . Oh, Herbert Hoover's staying there, too. Yeah, well, when are you coming over to see me? Now, now, now, listen, you bald-headed son of a bitch, don't get started on that Israel thing again, or I won't let you in the front door. . . . Well, no, I'll get to it as soon as I can. Well, Eddie, look now, stop crying, *just stop crying!* Eddie, every time you get on that Israel thing, you start to cry. I just can't do things in this job as fast as you think I should, Eddie. I've got a lot of other customers to think about. No, I can't invite Chaim Weizmann down to the White House. Israel isn't a state, yet, you know that. Wait a minute, I've got to do things by protocol in this job—you know, flags, invi . . . what flag? Well, what flag can the Waldorf Astoria be flying for Chaim Weizmann? I'll check with the State Department. All right, you get over here in about an hour, Eddie, and we'll have a nice chat. But Eddie, don't get into that Middle East thing, and don't start crying or I'll have you thrown out. . . . Good-bye.

He flips the intercom key.

President Truman visits with Eddie Jacobson

Rose, would you have General Vaughan check with the State Department and see what we have to do to get Chaim Weizmann invited down here? . . . Oh, and find out what flag the Waldorf Astoria in New York is flying and we'll fly the same damn thing. And listen, Rose, tell General Vaughan if the State Department kicks up any fuss about Weizmann not being a head of state, just tell them to forget it. We'll sneak him in the East Gate and keep it to ourselves.

He starts to walk stage center.

That man,

Pointing to the telephone:

that man that just called—Eddie Jacobson, an old friend of mine—he and I went bankrupt together back in Kansas City many years ago, and I've always felt that he was what this country is really all about. Eddie is always looking to do something for somebody, even though he might need the help more than they do. I've always felt there was enough for everybody in this country if the vested few could just get it out of their heads that all benefits ought to filter downward. I've always felt that one of the biggest problems we had in this country was that the financial control was in the hands of so very few. I have been saying that for a number of years and I believe the first time I said it publicly was on the floor of the United States Senate in 1937. . . .

12

He walks stage right and sits at the senate desk. He
opens his portfolio and takes out some notes which
he refers to.

Mr. President.

He is acknowledged by the Chair.

Thank you, Mr. President. Mr. President,
distinguished colleagues, just a few words this
morning. I . . . I . . . I want to say that I think one of
the chief difficulties in this country today is that we
worship money instead of honor. That's right, a
billionaire is much greater in the eyes of the people
than the public servant who works for the public
interest. It seems to make no difference that that
billionaire rode to his wealth on the sweat of little
children and the blood of underpaid labor. We seem
to forget that the Carnegie libraries are steeped in
the blood of the Homestead steel workers. . . .

Another Senator tries to get the floor.

No, I will not yield the floor. No, Mr. President.
Please, I . . . thank you, Mr. President. . . . I'll yield
when I'm ready. Just a moment. . . . And we do not
remember that the Rockefeller Foundation was
founded on the bodies of the dead miners of the
Colorado Iron and Fuel Company. In a word, we
worship mammon. Now, Wall Street with its ability
to control the wealth of this country and to hire the

13

best law brains, has yet to produce one financial statesman—by that I mean a man who can recognize the danger of this bigness and this concentration of wealth and try to do something about it. Instead, Wall Street still employs the best law brains to serve greed and selfish interests and I think . . . wait a minute . . . no! . . . Sir! . . . Now, I want to say very clearly that I think, one day, there's going to be a settlement because the unrest and unemployment in this country today, in my opinion, is a direct result of this concentration of wealth and the people are going to demand a settlement because there's going to be one receivership too many and one unnecessary depression too many. The people can stand just so much. Mr. President, we are building a Tower of Babel.

He returns to his desk and sits.

I yield the floor. . . .

The office buzzer is heard from his intercom. He walks to the desk in the Oval Office and flips it on. He listens to an imaginary voice.

Mr. Hoover's here? Good. I'll be right there.

He flips off the intercom, goes to the door leading to the outer office, and opens it.

Come in, Mr. President, come in.

14

He extends his hand and shakes the hand of the imaginary Herbert Hoover.

Good to see you, sir. How are you? Fine. Well, you are looking very well. Have a seat, sir. Oh . . . well, I'm sorry about that, "Mr. President." I don't know why I keep saying that. Well, it's the same—please sit down—same way with General Marshall. I could call the man George, but for some reason he's always "General" to me. Well, you are looking extremely well and it's nice to see you this morning. I wanted to talk to you, just for a moment if I might, about something that I believe you know more about than any man on this earth, and that's the subject of hunger. Now, we've got a surplus of food in this country, and I would like very much to try to get it to the right places in Europe and Asia, where it will help with this starvation business. You did a great job after World War I, feeding all those poor unfortunates, and I wondered if you'd consider doing such a job for us again right now.

He looks at Hoover and is taken aback by what he sees: Hoover has tears in his eyes.

What is it, did I say something, Mr. President? . . . I, well, no, heavens alive. No, Presidents have a right to a little emotion, just like anybody else. . . . You'll do it? Well, thank you. When could you start? Tomorrow, well, that suits me just fine, Mr. Hoover. The kind of help you can give us you can't just find anywhere, and I'm most grateful to you, sir. I'll send a car first thing in the morning. Oh, Mr. Hoover, you're welcome to stay in the White House if you

15

care to. Well, if you would rather stay in a hotel, I understand. Oh, say, speaking of hotels, you must know the folks that run the Waldorf Astoria rather well, living there and all. I may need your help in getting a flag of theirs . . . That's right, if my striped-pants boys can't handle it, I may call on you. . . . All right, sir, fine, I'll see you tomorrow morning.

He escorts Hoover out of the office.

You know, there goes one reason why I believe that Congress should enact legislation designating ex-Presidents honorary members of Congress. They'd have the same right as every legislator except the right to vote, and in that way, we would get the benefit of their judgments on things that are important. It seems to me it is just a waste of a great natural resource. Of course, we would have to limit the ex-Presidents' right to filibuster, particularly if they were members of the opposition party. But you know, if some of us old birds got to filibustering, you'd have to have a physician in attendance. It's amazing what this job of mine does to doctors. It seems to me that a man no sooner gets his hand off of the Bible and every doctor in the country wants to get down to Washington to be the President's physician. I gave the job to the one man who simply didn't want it, Wallace Graham. But I only got Wally because I promised him that he would have all of Walter Reed Hospital to operate on.

President Truman with Former President Herbert Hoover

He sits at his desk.

One time I was ailing, and the word must have
gotten out because Wally Graham got a call from a
very famous doctor, a man named Chevalier
Jackson, from the Temple Medical School in
Philadelphia, Pennsylvania. He invented a thing
called a bronchoscope—that's a tube that you put
down people's throats and then you can search
around in their chest area. Well, he and his staff
were just beside themselves to get down to
Washington to give me what they call a
bronchoscopy. He called Wally. Well, Wally didn't
want to insult the eminent doctor, so he put him on
hold, in the outer office, and he came in and told me.
And I said, "Wally, did you tell him what my
problem was?" He said that he didn't have a chance,
that the doctor was practically on the plane down
here, so I had the call switched in here to me.

He picks up the phone.

Dr. Jackson? Harry Truman. . . . I'm all right. I guess
I'm holding my own in the world. Doctor . . . say,
Doctor, I know you're a busy man. You'd probably
like to now get the story from the horse's mouth. . . .
You would. Well, all right. Now I don't know how
you fellows work, but I'm sure before you start on a
journey, you'd like to know where you're going. . . .
You would, well, I'm sure you want to have that tube
of yours pointed in the right direction. Doctor, if you
can point it at my other end I would be happy to

18

have you take a peek, 'cause what I got is just good old-fashioned diarrhea. Dr. Jackson . . . Dr. Jackson, are you there? That was the last we heard from the eminent doctor.

He hangs up the phone and walks stage center.

I suppose the man who suffered the most real physical pain in this office would have been Thomas Jefferson. Jefferson suffered from excruciating migraine headaches. He had a real problem—between his heart and his mind. He was in constant conflict about what he had written in the Constitution—because during his presidency, he did virtually nothing to destroy the institution of slavery, which he fervently believed should be abolished. His migraines ended only when he left the presidency. He lived his own private civil war for the rest of his life, which probably only ended with his death.

Reciting:

His life was gentle, and the elements
So mix'd in him that Nature might stand up
And say to all the world, This was a man!

He walks back to his desk.

You know, I don't believe that a day goes by in this office that I don't sometime or other think how FDR might be running the store.

19

*He becomes aware of Roosevelt's ghost sitting in
one of the chairs.*

Oh, oh, yes, Mr. Roosevelt, you're a tough man to
follow. More than once I have heard myself referred
to as "His Accidency." How do I like the job? Well,
the pay's pretty good. There's certainly lots to do. Of
course, no matter what you do, there's always some
son of a bitch who won't like it. It's the hottest
kitchen in the world, I'd expect. Cigarette?

*He looks for some on his person, Finds none, then
digs into his desk.*

Well, I don't use them myself, but I must have some
here for visiting ex-Presidents. Wait a minute, here
we are. All right, there. You know my Surgeon
General tells me that these things may be causing
lung cancer and a lot more that are killing people
these days.

He laughs.

That's right, it won't hurt you now, will it? . . .
Churchill? Winston Churchill, in my opinion, sir, is a
great statesman, a gentleman. . . . Stalin? Well,
there's another cup of tea. One thing that I will say
about old Uncle Joe, though, he is a very industrious,
dedicated, and creative liar. When I went to Potsdam
to meet him, I, well, you know how it is, I got all

TOP: A stroll with Winston Churchill

BOTTOM: The "Big Three" at Potsdam (before the British election)

20

decked out, trussed up in my tuxedo, preacher coat, my high hat, low hat, and hard hat. Hard hats are mandatory when you're negotiating with the Russians, as you well know. Anyway, while we were there, Stalin drank vodka during the entire time, and I marveled at the man's ability to hold his liquor. About the fourth day at about three o'clock in the afternoon, I reached over, picked up his glass, and I took a sip—white wine!

He laughs.

The bomb? . . . Well, you know, of course, that I didn't know we even had the damn thing until you left us and Secretary Stimson came in and briefed me on it.

He sits opposite FDR's ghost. He is very serious.

I learned that it worked the day after I got to Potsdam and I told Stalin about it. He just shrugged his shoulders like he had known about it all along, which the son of a bitch probably did. Winston Churchill said I had no choice, had to drop it immediately and end the war. My military people told me that we could expect over a million casualties on both sides if we tried to invade the mainland of Japan. . . . Options? Well, I didn't have any options. We dropped the bomb and heard nothing, so we dropped the second one and they capitulated. . . . Did it bother me?

He thinks on this—it did bother him.

Well, Mr. Roosevelt, let me tell you something. If I had to make the same decision tomorrow, I would do the same damn thing if I thought it would end the war. And let me say something else. I have been patiently waiting for somebody to apologize for Pearl Harbor. It was terrible that you weren't able to be there to sign the final Potsdam communiqué. . . . Well, thank you. Incredible, I couldn't believe it either, that Churchill'd be voted out of office in the middle of a major war by that little bird, Attlee. Yes, Churchill took it rather hard, but he never lost his touch. When he heard about the election results he said, "Harry, remember one thing about Clement Attlee—there's a lot less there than meets the eye." I laughed and said he seemed like a modest little guy to me, and he said, "Well, he's got lots to be modest about."

They both have a laugh.

Am I going to run again? Hell, I haven't run yet.

Roosevelt disappears. Truman walks out of the Oval Office. He takes off his jacket and tie, opens his shirt collar, and rolls up his sleeves.

You know, sometimes the pressures in this office get just a little "borderline." Now, when that happens I always try to get home to Independence, Missoura, every chance I can. I really think that it's the isolation in that room that does it, and I seem to lose touch with people. When that happens, as I say, I run home and try and, well, sort of pull things down to size, I guess. But I do a lot less pulling than I do pushing this blamed lawn mower.

He takes the lawn mower and starts to mow, politely bowing to supposed people as they pass his mother-in-law's house at 120 Delaware Avenue.

Morning. . . . Morning. . . . Nice to see you. Ah, well, it's nice to be home on such a lovely weekend. . . . Sue Gentry, how are you, Sue?

He tries to shake hands with Sue through an imaginary fence.

Well, I don't, let's, ah, let's do it this way. Oh, yes, you know, these things, the Secret Service put the blamed thing in. . . . What am I doing mowing the lawn on Sunday? Well, the Boss asked me to do the lawn. . . . Well, grass grows on Sunday the same as any other day. If I were on wages, I'd be on overtime. . . . You've got to go to church, well, of course you do, Sue. Have a good pray.

As Sue Gentry leaves, his head turns toward the house and he shouts out:

I got to mow the lawn!!

---

120 North Delaware Avenue, Independence, Missouri (fence courtesy of U. S. Secret Service)

To the audience:

You know, I've found that if you really don't want to do something, do it on Sunday. That way the Boss will think you've tarnished the Sabbath and she'll never ask you to do it again. You'll see, it'll work out that way. I've always been a "lightfoot" Baptist myself. Most of my family were Baptists—they thought the Baptists had the inside track to happiness after the grave. My favorite relative was my Grandfather Solomon Young. He was a very independent man and he hated hypocrites. I remember him saying to me when I was just a boy, "Harry," he said, "if you ever run into a man who howls too long on Saturday night and prays too loud on Sunday morning, go home and lock your smoke house." I found that out when I had my first job at Jim Clinton's drugstore down on the square. When I was just a kid, I used to go into Jim Clinton's drugstore very early in the morning, sweep up, and wash out the medicine bottles. It was quite an education for me to see how many of the anti-saloon leaguers, the churchgoers, would come in to get an eye opener in the morning. Jim charged them about ten cents an ounce, and he kept it back in the prescription department. Before they'd leave, they'd peep out a little hole to make sure that nobody had seen them. Well, it was my first brush with phoneys, and I've never had any use for them since. I've always favored the rough old boys. If they wanted to knock back a few, they just walked into any saloon down on the square. I never felt that any real man had to hide behind a bunch of test tubes when he wanted to strike a blow for liberty. Of course, there are three things on this earth that'll ruin a man—

26

power, money, and women. If a man can accept power as a temporary thing, he's going to be all right. But if he thinks he's the cause of the power, that'll ruin him. And money, if a man makes too much money too quickly, it can separate him from the rest of the human race who have to work most of their lives just to earn a living. And if a man is disloyal to his family, well, that'll ruin him. 'Cause if you've got the right partner in life, well, you're not going to have much trouble. But, if you're just looking to get some honey on your stinger, then you're in one hell of a fix, anyway. If you read your history, you'll find I'm right.

He takes off his glasses and cleans them.

I've had to wear these blamed things all my life. I had a case of diphtheria when I was ten years old, almost ruined my eyesight. I wasn't very athletic as a boy. Now, the Boss, Bess, is the real tomboy in the family. She used to play baseball with the kids and I, well, they never let me play. I had to umpire. Bess could out-whistle any kid on the block. And I want to tell you something else about the Boss. She's very modest about her accomplishments, you know. She was shotput champion of Independence High School. Now that's the truth. My mother got me interested in the piano and reading. She was a very gentle woman. Her name was Martha. She was very artistic, very musical, and she was a college graduate. She flaunted the Baptists by attending dances. She was a real lightfoot Baptist. My father, John Truman, was a very short, feisty man who used to like to knock people's hats off when they weren't looking. They called him the "Bantam Cock." He had absolutely no interest at all in book learning. He quit school at a very early age and told his father that he wanted to become a mule trader. Well, Grandfather Truman said it wasn't a very lofty position for a man to aspire to, but if he had his heart set on it to go ahead, tell the truth, and nobody'd believe him. My mother wanted me to attend college, but my father suffered some financial setbacks, so I was unable to do so. I went to timekeeping for the Santa Fe Railroad.

Offstage a screendoor is opened.

Oh, oh, I believe the women are about to deliver me from my bondage.

He faces the imaginary Bess.

Well, yes, Boss, what is it? What? I embarrassed your mother? How did I do that? But, Bess, you asked me to mow the lawn. She's really on the war path, is she. . . . Oh, dear, I'm sorry, Bess, I wouldn't have done it if I'd known that. . . . Well, she's not on that again. Oh, for heaven's sake, Bess, just tell her I'm going to run, will you? If I can't beat Tom Dewey . . . Look, would you try this, Bess, just try. Tell her that I'm going to win. All right, yes, I'll bring the mower in right away. You bet I will, Boss. All right.

John and Martha Truman

*He's delighted by his triumph as he faces the
audience.*

What did I tell you? It never fails. You know, her
mother, Madge Gates Wallace, well, she was known
as the most stylish woman in Independence,
Missoura. And her father, Porterfield Gates, made a
sizable fortune milling Queen of the Pantry Flour. I
know I'm not exactly what she had in mind for a
son-in-law, but that's all right. If she never did
anything in her life but have Bess, that's good
enough for me. You all know the old expression:
"Behind every successful man is a proud wife, and a
surprised mother-in-law." But she's a pistol.
Honestly, she's got a mind of her own. I remember
when the Secret Service put this fence around the
house.

He indicates the fence in front of him.

Now, it's Mother Wallace's house, you know, and
when she saw it, I tell you the manure hit the fan.
Well, she said, "Nobody, I don't care who it is,
nobody on this earth is going to put a fence around
my house without my permission. I don't care if it's
the government, the President, or who it is!" She
finally simmered down, but I'll tell you, every time
she goes through that gate right there, this fence
cringes.

He laughs at the idea.

I once asked John Snyder, my secretary of the
treasury, what this thing cost. He said about fifteen
hundred dollars. Sounds like a lot of money, doesn't

'It's My Own Version Of Harry Truman's Slogan'

Wed., Feb. 7, 1973

ST. LOUIS POST-DISPATCH

it? Well, you know a fella could get rich in this job, if he really wanted to, but I found out something a long time ago—when you play ball with the money boys, *you* pay! Oh, I've done some favors for friends down through the years, just like any other influence peddler in Washington, but I never got anything for myself out of it. And, I'll tell you something else. No man can get rich in politics unless he's a crook! It can't be done. I got into politics in a rather strange way, through the military. I was in the National Guard just before World War I and one of my fellow officers was named Jim Pendergast. Now, Jim and I became very good friends, and if I hadn't met Jim Pendergast, I wouldn't be in this job today. Before I went overseas, I inherited an artillery outfit called Battery D.

He puts on a helmet and army jacket.

They were known as the "Dizzy D's" and they were known as the "Dizzy D's" because they were the wildest, hardest-drinking bunch of Irishmen that ever staggered around the streets of Kansas City. They had two officers before me. One of them was discharged from the service because he couldn't handle the "Dizzy D's" and the other one had a nervous breakdown. Well, I'll never forget the first day I met that bunch. They were waiting for me. Of course, they expected me to chew them out. Well, I fooled them.

He faces the "Dizzy D."

Dismissed! Except the noncoms.

The infamous Battery D

I said, except the noncoms. Boys, they tell me that your outfit is known as the "Dizzy D." Well, the "D" has got to stand for "dumb" because that's exactly what you are. All you've done since you've been in France is fight among yourselves, drink, and go to mass. I don't think there's a real fighter in this outfit. You're going to have to get along with me because from now on every one of you is going to be responsible for the discipline in his squad and section. And if any one of you think you can't handle it, well, speak up right now, and I'll punch you right in the nose! Dismissed. We got along, in fact, they did very well. However, there was one day that I'll never forget. . . . We were pinned down by German artillery fire. One of my sergeants panicked and headed for the rear, and before I knew it, my entire battery was on the run. Well, right then and there I learned the greatest counteroffensive weapon in warfare—CUSSIN'! Come back here, you dirty mackerel snappers. You dirty yellow Irish sons of bitches, get back here. Up your Irish asses! You're not Irish, you're acting like a bunch of goddamn Limeys. Go hide under the Queen's skirts! Yes, I'm talking about you, Walsh, and you, McNeil, all you Irish bastards. Don't come at me, Walsh! Don't come at me—there are the Krauts! Get on the guns! Get on the guns! Fire at will. Up the Irish. UP THE IRISH!!!

Suddenly it all stops.

We called that the Battle of Who Run! . . .

34

He removes his helmet and jacket.

When I got back from France, I married Bess. Her mother had some misgivings about it, but we went ahead and did it. In fact, we moved into Mother Wallace's house, where we've lived ever since. When I was courting Bess, I wrote her a silo full of letters. One day after I was President, I came into the living room, and I found Bess down on her knees by the fireplace burning the letters. I said she oughtn't to do it, and she said, "Why not, I've read them." I said, "Bess, think of history." She said, "I am," and she kept right on burning.

He walks to an old-fashioned roll-top type desk. On it is a bow tie. He puts it on and sits at the desk.

Shortly after I got back from the war, I ran into Eddie Jacobson, and on a handshake we decided to go into business together. We opened a haberdashery store. Some of our buddies from Battery D, including Jim Pendergast, would stop in from time to time and we'd swap lies about how we won the war. Eddie and I did pretty well until the Depression of 1922 hit and we had to go out of business. Eddie went out on the road selling shirts. Before I could get any kind of a job, I found myself running for county judge in Jackson County. Now, that isn't a proper judge—it's more of a county commissioner in Missoura. I had the political backing of the Pendergast machine, and of course, I'd gotten that because Tom Pendergast had been told by Jim that I was one officer in the war whose men didn't want to shoot him. So, I found myself in my old beat-up Dodge running all over the

35

place fighting what was a new war for me, a war where you "shoot from the lip." I think I got elected because I had more relatives in the county than anybody else. And, of course, I was broke, and since most folks were broke, too, they naturally went for a fellow who was in the same fix. My first job after I got elected was building roads. We had more mud roads in Jackson County at that time than any other county in America. Now, when you start talking road-building, it's as though you were a female moth who just released her entire load of bombykol all in one spray. Immediately, you would have at least a trillion males headed in your direction. Well, those males are called "road contractors," and I got my first taste of them when Tom Pendergast paid me a visit after the bond issue had been passed to build the roads.

Pendergast and three road builders have entered Truman's office.
Very unsure of himself:

Well, Mr. Pendergast, all right, Tom. . . . You bet, fine, yes, Tom, no, I don't. . . . Ross, yes, fine, nice to know you. No, sir, I don't know them. No, but I've, well, heard of them. Well, well, Tom, what can I do for you, sit down. For heaven's sake, sit down. Yes, yes, Tom, what? Yes, I know. I know they're your supporters, but I got to tell you, I don't believe

---

TOP: Harry and Bess in the front seat of his 1912 Stafford
BOTTOM: Truman & Jacobson, Haberdashers

37

they're very good road-builders, and that's all that really concerns me. Well, their bids were too damn high, Tom, and the roads they build, well, they're pie-crust road-builders. By that I mean the roads they build are crumbling like pie-crusts. I've seen them. . . . I know they pay taxes here, Tom, but that doesn't entitle them to the money. I'm going to award the job to some bunch from out of state. Their bids are lower, and the roads they build hold up. I know that because I've seen them.

The three contractors rise as though to leave.

Oh, gentlemen, you're leaving. So soon? All right, fine, boys, come around anytime, it's the same for everybody.

He watches them leave and then turns to Tom:

Well, Tom, that's the way it is. I'm not going to say I'm sorry. No, no, Mr. Pendergast, that's all right. I guess you don't know me very well, and . . . no, I don't think I'm being contrary, I think I'm being businesslike. At least, I hope I am. . . . No. I don't think you're interfering. Let's just say it's the beginning of an understanding. All right, all right, Mr. Pender . . . Tom, all right, fine, I'll do just that. I'll do what I think is right.

He watches Pendergast leave.

Truman and Tom Pendergast

38

Shortly after that, it came out that Pendergast was a secret partner of those three men, and he lost a considerable amount of money by my decision. But he did not interfere with my work at that time, or at any other time, even when he was in deep trouble and needed money desperately. And in 1940 I had to decide whether I was going to run for a second term. I wanted to, but things were very bleak for me because the Pendergast machine had fallen apart completely. Tom Pendergast had been indicted for income tax evasion and sent to prison, and the leader of my own party, President Franklin Delano Roosevelt, was against me because I was backing legislation in the Senate to limit the election of presidents to two terms. Roosevelt, of course, was really planning to run for a third term, and he decided to back a man named Lloyd Stark, who was the then governor of Missoura. Stark had all the influential Democrats behind him. He had all the big money boys in the state, and he had the support of the newspapers, save one, which led me to believe that I had been doing a good job in the Senate. Well, I had two choices—I could fold my tent, or I could get off my ass and do something about it. I chose the latter. In fact, I wired Roosevelt that I was going to run even if I got one vote—*mine*! Now, as I say, Stark, my opponent, had everything. I thought I might be able to get the backing of labor because I supported some rather important pro-labor legislation in the Senate and I hoped the boys might remember that. I found out one thing—in union there is strength, and in unions more strength. However, I needed a good deal more than labor and I knew it. In fact, I needed every helping hand I could get in that election. Now, there comes a time in every man's life when he has to stand up to be counted, stand up and say what he really believes in. Of course, if it can be practical at the same time, so much the better. At that time in Missoura we had about two million mules, each one worth about ninety dollars, and we had two hundred forty-five thousand Negroes. Well, to a lot of people they weren't worth anything. They were wrong. It was wrong and I said so. I did it on the courthouse steps in Sedalia, Missoura, June 15, 1940. It was a very hot summer day and Sedalia was a stronghold of the Ku Klux Klan. There wasn't a black face in the crowd. . . .

He wipes his brow, and sets himself for something he's wanted to say a long time.

Friends and neighbors, can you hear me in the back? Howard, could you get up on something or move closer. I'll talk as loudly as I can. Friends, it won't be long. I'm not going to keep you here in this heat but a minute. I just wanted to get something off my chest, and then I'm going to move on. But before I do, I just wanted to say very simply, folks, that I believe in the brotherhood of man, and not just the brotherhood of white men.

He waves them down.

No, Howard, well, let me finish—would you please?— because I believe in the brotherhood of all men before the law. Oh, yes, I do and I think you do, well, you must, if you believe in the Bill of Rights and the

41

Constitution of the United States. Folks, in recent years, we all know here, every one of us knows, that the progress of the Negroes from the country to the city has been speeded up considerably, and that's due, of course, to the lynching, the beatings, and mob violence. Well, since they've gotten into the large cities, they've been virtually ignored. They've been forced into segregated slums. They don't have the necessities of life. They don't have any job opportunities and as free men, in my opinion, they're entitled to something better than that. . . . Wait a minute. Some of you I can see here don't quite agree with me, but you got to agree that if we push the Negro down into the depths of degradation, the white man is going to go down with him. Oh, yes, he is, because the law of compensation has got to apply. As Booker T. Washington said, "If you're going to hold a black man in the gutter, there has to be a white man in the gutter to hold him there.". . .

He walks out of Sedalia, at stage center.

I won that election by eight thousand votes. Now, we've made a lot of progress in civil rights since those days, I guess, but I still believe that the Negro has to walk a fine line in our society just to survive. I remember an old Negro back in Grandview, Missoura, many years ago, who told me that he had gotten a bottle of liquor from his boss. I asked him how it was. He said, "Well, just about right." I said, "What do you mean, 'just about right'?" He said, "Well, if it was any better, he wouldn't have given it to me, and if it was any worse, I wouldn't have drunk it." Of course, in those days, you know the Ku

Klux Klan was a real power in my part of the country. Oh, indeed they were, and in my campaign of 1924 they really figured very prominently. They were a rough bunch. Of course, they were only rough in a bunch. They were racists, and their philosophy was the ultimate in vulgarity.

He picks up a KKK hood.

This was their shield. Behind it they felt safe.

He exchanges the shield for the torch.

This is a torch. Its purpose is to give man light. In their hands, it was very often a witness to lynchings, beatings, and murders.

He lays the torch aside.

A bunch of the Klan boys came to my office, just before the election, and said they had a problem with me. They said they understood that my Grandfather, Solomon Young, was a Jew, but that they'd give me a special dispensation for that, and their support, if I would join them. Well, I looked at those miserable creatures and I said that my Grandfather Young was not a Jew, and that if he was I'd be proud to say so, and that they could take their support and stick it where the good Lord intended all such things to be stuck! We parted enemies . . . Thank God! Of course, if you stay in political life long enough, just about anything can happen to you. It usually does, but I think a man has to draw the line when his own life is threatened. And it came to that. The Klan threatened to kill me. Bess and I had just had our lovely little Margaret and it upset both of us. I knew there was only one way to handle it and that was *head* on!

He walks to a bale of hay.

The boys were having one of their pow-wows up at Lee's Summit that night, and I thought that just might be the place to confront them. I wanted to go up there alone, but Eddie Jacobson insisted on going with me. That was a very courageous thing for Eddie Jacobson to do because Eddie was one of the things they hated worse on this earth. Eddie was a Jew. . . .

He mounts the bale of hay, inwardly frightened, yet his stand is defiant.

Evening, boys. I understand that some of you threatened to kill me. Well, if you want to take your lives in your own hands, let's get on with it.

He looks at them hard.

So you're the yellow scum that's going to tell me who I can't hire—a black man, a Catholic, a Jew or anybody else I damn well please. Well, boys, being farm kin, you must know that that is pure, undiluted bullshit! That's what that is! I'm going to hire anybody I goddamn please! Because, boys, those jobs are for all the people and not just for a few hooded bastards like you! Shame on you! Shame on you!

44

Calling yourselves the Invisible Empire, why, the good Lord should strike you from the face of the earth!

Waits for something to happen—nothing.

I'm leaving you chosen people, but before I do, I want to tell you what Eddie Jacobson said on the way up here. Eddie said that whoever organized your courageous gang had to be a Jew, because only a Jew could sell you stupid idiots a dollar ninety-five nightshirt for sixteen dollars! Now, Eddie and I are going to go find a saloon and strike a blow for liberty! . . .

He gets off the bale of hay and walks stage center.

I lost that election. They beat me, but I was never prouder to lose anything in my entire life.

*From behind stage comes a loud finger whistle—
it's Bess calling.
Pointing in the direction of the whistle:*

Now there is the whistle that is the envy of every kid on this block. She can't put the shot any more, but she still has a whistle. That's my signal to stop talking with you this Sunday morning. I'm going to get an earful when I get inside, but, it sure beats cutting grass.

He exits.

The stage is dark. The singing voice of Margaret
Truman is heard. She sings Romberg's "One Kiss."
After the music is established, the lights go up,
revealing Truman at his desk in the Oval Office.

Mr. Paul Hume, music critic, *Washington Post,*
Washington, D.C. Mr. Hume: I've just read your
review of my daughter Margaret's concert last night
and I've come to the conclusion that you're an
eight-ulcer man on four-ulcer pay. And after reading
such poppycock, it's obvious that you're off the beam
and that at least four of your ulcers are working
overtime. I hope to meet you and when I do, you're
going to need a new nose, plenty of beef steak for
black eyes, and perhaps a jock strap below. . . .

He looks in his wallet for a stamp, finds none, and
flips the intercom key.

Rose, would you bring in a couple of three-cent
stamps, please? No lectures on my franking
privileges, Rose, just bring in the stamps. Oh, and
bring your book, too, Rose. Thank you.

To the audience:

Well, this is the kind of day that started out with all
the right things happening to make it all go wrong.

A musical performance by Margaret Truman

The first thing this morning, I got the communiqués from Korea, and we're doing very badly over there. Then I had to tell Margaret about the death of our dear, dear, beloved Charlie Ross. He died unexpectedly at his desk yesterday. He was Margaret's very special and wonderful friend. When I had to announce it to the press, I broke down and cried like a baby, and then I had to read this damn thing.

Pointing to the Washington Post:

You know it seems to me that sometimes these critic fellows are just a little rough. But I was a father before I became President, and I'm going to be a father when I leave this office, so that's the way it's going to be—Mr. Hume, *you son of a bitch!*

Rose enters.

No, no, not you, Rose, for heaven sakes, no. Thank you, Rose. Oh, would you sit down, please. I want to dictate a few short notes here. First, one goes to some bird in Louisiana. He's a congressman named Aber. . . . Herbert, that's right, yeah, H-E-R-B-E-R-T, all right, fine, ah. . . . Dear Congressman: Yesterday one of my aides brought me a memo that you had made a statement to the effect that you wanted the churches to set aside one day a week to ask the good Lord to be my guidance and wisdom. Well, Congressman, while I am very grateful for your concern for me and for your possible influence with the Almighty, from what I know of the Man, he's got a hell of a lot more important things to do. Sign it God's humble servant—Harry S. Truman. . . .

He looks at Rose.

Oh, you want to cut "hell of a lot." Fine, Rose, if it makes it easier for you. The next one is to Senator Bishop, of Colorado.

Looking through his mail:

Here it is. . . . Dear Senator: Not only would I not appoint John L. Lewis ambassador to the Soviet Union, I wouldn't appoint the old bastard dog catcher! . . . I know you want to cut out "old bastard." . . . You don't. You want to cut "dog catcher"? . . . Oh, you do. Well, what about postmaster general? That'd be just as bad.

He chuckles.

All right, Rose. Leave it as it is.

He picks up the phone.

Hackie, get me Sam Rayburn, would you please? You know, Rose, there's a story going around these days about me here in Washington. Some old party hen is supposed to have come up to Bess and said, "Mrs. Truman, can't you get the President to stop using the word 'manure'?" And Bess is supposed to have replied, "It's taken me forty years to get him to use it." That's the kind of answer I'd hope the Boss might give. . . . Sam? Harry. Say listen, Sam.

He waves Rose out.

I'm getting a lot of pressure from those oil boys down your way. That's . . . yeah, well, Sam, there's no . . . they're trying to get their hands on the Tideland Oil Reserves, and there's no way in hell they're going to do it. . . . Why, of course not, they'd wind up selling it right back to the government and we'd pay through the nose for something we already own. Well, just tell them that there's no sale. Oh, Sam, when are you coming over to see me? Well, I got a new supply of turkey nip. Remember, there's only one thing worse than a drinking man—one who doesn't.

He hangs up and walks stage center.

You know, when you're in this, job you've got to keep your eye on the money hungry. Why, if they had their way, they'd scar this country from one end to the other if they had a bulldozer big enough. Why, we'd wind up with just a bunch of neon-lighted junkyards, billboards—concrete America. Anything for a buck! Ugly squalor's what it would be. Of course, ugliness is what drags us down. Beauty, of course, lifts us up. You know, whenever I've really despaired of the human race, and I do from time to time, I always go and take a look at fellows like Frans Hals, Rubens, and da Vinci. I guess my favorite would be Rembrandt. Of course, I suppose the ugliest invention of mankind would be war. There's no question about that. You know everybody has a bad time in war, and presidents are no exceptions. They not only get hell from the enemy, but they catch it from their own generals. I certainly had trouble with one of my generals. Oh, yes, I did. He couldn't get it through his bullet-proof head that, as Clemenceau once said, "War is much too serious a matter to be left to generals." Now, Lincoln certainly had problems with one of his generals. *His* general was McClellan. McClellan was a very interesting man. He had been president of some Illinois railroad before the war, and Lincoln as a young lawyer had worked for McClellan. When Lincoln became President, McClellan could not accept the fact that Lincoln was no longer an employee. In fact, McClellan acted more like President than the President, but McClellan suffered from conceit, which is God's gift to little men. Lincoln was much too big a man, of course, to be troubled by McClellan's fantasies. He once said that McClellan reminded him of the fellow whose horse got to kicking around and got his hoof caught in the stirrup and the fellow looked down and said, "Look here, you want to get on, I'll get off." I've always found it easy to see why the military sometimes finds it difficult to understand the workings of a free government. They've always lived a regimented, dictatorial kind of life. The military was never intended to be a debating society. If you want to talk, get into politics. There's plenty to say, if you've got something to say, or even if you don't have anything to say. It's amazing how many guys, the less they say, the longer they stay! But I have no objection, of course, to the military getting into politics. It's just that the generals sometimes feel that they want to start at the top, and we're sometimes damn fools enough to let them do just that. My general, *Douglas MacArthur,* now, MacArthur'd been out of the country for fourteen long years and we all know how tall a man can grow in that length of time. I always had the greatest respect for Douglas MacArthur's military ability, and I even understood the role he was playing for the Orientals—that of Diety. But I simply could not permit him to disregard and disobey the decisions and instructions of the American government, *your elected government.* Of course, our problems with MacArthur started long before Korea. Oh, yes, they started right after Japan surrendered. MacArthur thought that all policy relative to Japan should originate in Tokyo, with him, and not in Washington. He made pronouncements all the time about our occupational policies without checking with the government first. And I've got to tell you honestly that it became rather embarrassing, to say the least, as President of the United States, to find out what we were doing in the morning newspaper.

Intercom buzzes.

Yes, Rose. Tell the General I'll be right there. Well, now that's General Marshall waiting out there. He's a very punctual man, but this morning he is one half hour early. I gave him some communiqués to read

---

Presenting an Oak Leaf Cluster to General George C. Marshall

last night that I had exchanged with MacArthur over the past few years. Well, I've said some harsh things here, about the military, but I want to tell you that the man sitting in the outer office is one of the most dedicated Americans I've ever been privileged to know. Omar Bradley's another one. General Bradley is one of the finest, most brilliant field commanders this country has ever produced. And both those gentlemen have been deeply involved with me in this entire Korean operation, and all of us have been deeply concerned that the conflict might erupt into World War III.

He opens the door for Marshall.

Come in, General. . . . Yes, sir, come on in. Have a chair. . . . Oh, you prefer to stand, all right, sir, fine.

He sits. His eyes follow Marshall as the General paces the room.

Well, General, what do you think of the communi . . . Yes, I know, they're incredible, aren't they. I agree. . . . Absolutely, oh, yes. Oh, sure. Well, Acheson says we've just got to show MacArthur, *once and for all,* who the President of the United States is. . . . Harriman? He agrees, too. I know, *force, force, force,* that's all he wants. That's all he keeps pushing for. I think that Mark Clark said it best of all when he said that "force did not mean to shoot the works, but rather to see that the enemy attack failed." . . . So you would have fired him two years ago if you'd

President Truman with General Omar Bradley

known then what you know now? What about Bradley? Would you ask him, please? Right now, General, and let me know what he says.

Marshall leaves.

I don't know how we got to this stage. I really don't know. I probably never will. It seems to me, at any rate, that I have done everything in my power to try to communicate with General MacArthur. Why, I even flew sixteen thousand miles to Wake Island. I felt it was absolutely imperative that we clear the air between us.

He walks stage center.

Well, when I got there, there he was, circling the island, waiting for me to land first. He said they had some mechanical trouble, but I knew what he was up to. He was play acting. He's quite a play actor, you know. So, I had my pilot tell his pilot to get that damn plane on the ground and they did. Their mechanical difficulty cleared up miraculously. Now, as I was saying, he was a play actor. He was waiting for me. There he was with the battered cap, the sunglasses, the pipe, and the unbuttoned shirt.

He removes his jacket.

But I have never believed in dressing down a man in front of people. I tell you, no matter what a man has done that's wrong, if you take his dignity away from him, well, he's got nothing left.

He slings his jacket over his shoulder and starts his walk on the beach.

56

So, I suggested that MacArthur and I take a walk along the beach alone.

To MacArthur:

General, you know, I really don't much care what you think of me as Harry Truman. Wait a minute, General . . . but, I do, I do care what you think of me as President of the United States because, *goddamn it, that's what I am!!!* Now, the folks back home elected me to this office, and they expect me to be the boss. And as long as a frog is a reptile with edible legs, that's exactly what I mean to be. . . . Wait a minute, General MacArthur. You've got to stop this talk about going into China and this reinvolving Chiang Kai-Shek is absolutely absurd. Why, his troops couldn't fight their way out of a Hong Kong whorehouse! And, you know what would happen if they got back in this thing? Why, he and that Madame of his . . . well, I'll tell you what would happen. They would use it as an excuse to rob us blind again. . . . Yes, I said "again"! Why, they've stolen two billion of the thirty billion we've already given them! You didn't know that? Well, it's high time you did, General. And another thing, you've got to stop making these damn statements that are inflaming that China lobby back in the country. Because I'm sick and tired of having that goddamn Jenner and McCarthy, and that little bird from California, whatever his name is, calling my administration a bunch of Commies. It's got to stop! Those men are dangerous liars. They're the enemies of freedom! They're a bunch of reckless fanatics who could destroy us all! We've got a big enough job trying to keep this whole damn thing from blowing

57

up in all our faces. . . . Well, all right. Now are the Chinese going to intervene? . . . They're not. Well, do you see any massive buildup up there at all? . . . You don't . . . General, and if they do intervene? . . . You could cope with it. . . . They'd be inviting a slaughter? Well, all right, General, that's got to be good enough for me.

He puts his jacket on and addresses the audience.

He said he was going to have the boys home by Christmas. Well, of course, he neglected to check with the Chinese, and Christmas, meaning absolutely nothing to them, is when they attacked. They came across the border by the thousands, and to put it very bluntly, they kicked the living hell out

58

of us. Of course, MacArthur announced publicly that he could have won it if I'd let him do what he wanted to do. Well, we almost lost Korea, but we hung on and finally we were able to turn the Eighth Army around in a counteroffensive. But we had learned one very important lesson—if we had let MacArthur force or talk us into a large-scale military operation on the mainland of China, it would have been a disaster for all of us, except, of course, the Russians, who were the true aggressors. So, slowly and very painfully and at a great cost of life, we inched our way on the Korean peninsula, and it looked as though an armistice might be in sight. In fact, I instituted ceasefire negotiations through the United Nations. We thought we might be able to contain the thing, but that *voice* in Tokyo, MacArthur, despite repeated instructions to talk *to me first,* talked to everybody but me. He called for a blockade of the China mainland. He wanted to bomb her industrial centers. Well, there I was, the President of the United States, trying to negotiate a ceasefire with the enemy, while one of my subordinates was calling for an all-out attack on them. *And, listen to this,* while we were involved, *deeply* involved, in that painful ceasefire negotiation through the United Nations, at the same time, unilaterially, General MacArthur was calling for the North Koreans *to surrender to him personally!* I could not continue to allow this insubordination to go on. Had I done so, I would have surrendered the civilian control of your government to the military, and, *I was not about to do that!* And, of course, the last straw came when MacArthur wrote a letter to Joseph Martin, House Minority Leader. Joe Martin read it on the floor of the House, and in that letter, MacArthur accused my administration . . . he said that my administration should be indicted for the murder of thousands of American boys. If we were not in Korea to win . . . well, the point was, that we weren't in Korea to win anything! We were in Korea to stop something, namely aggression! The United Nations' forces were there for one reason, *to preserve the peace of the world for all mankind.*

The phone rings. He answers it.

Yes, oh, yes, General Marshall, Bradley agrees. All right, fire the son of a bitch!

He hangs up. Pensive:

It bothered me. It bothered me very much. There

60

was never any doubt in my mind that MacArthur was for America. We all were for America. Isn't it amazing, though, how this old country seems to survive even though some of her people go at her, sometimes, with a meat ax, always in the name of trying to preserve her. You see, MacArthur's problem was that he could never understand that his fight was not with Harry Truman. His fight was with the President of the United States. He could never see that it had any constitutional significance at all. Of course, shortly thereafter, I got into a constitutional briar patch myself when I wanted to take over the steel mills in a labor dispute. I thought that closing them would hurt our Korean war effort. Well, the Supreme Court said that I had no constitutional right to do so, none whatsoever, and I got brought down just like anybody else. War or no war, the Constitution prevailed. And that's as it should be. *The law is for everybody in this country!* Of course, all administrations have their law breakers, and mine was no exception. I had some bad apples. Fortunately, they were little ones. And when they were caught, they were out in the street. Now, politics is a rough game—very rough at times, but I believe that there's a world of difference between rough and dirty. I'll give you an example. I'm sure you all know about that letter that Eisenhower wrote to General Marshall right after the war when he wanted to come back to the States, leave his wife, and marry that Englishwoman. All right, well . . . Marshall brought it here and showed it to me. Marshall thought it was a stupid thing for Ike to do and I concurred. So, Marshall wrote a letter to Ike to that effect, and that should have been the end of it, but it wasn't. In 1952, when Eisenhower finally

61

decided he wanted to be a Republican and was going to seek the nomination of that party for the presidency, some of Robert Taft's people—now, I want to say that I never thought, for one minute, that Robert Taft knew anything about this. I had the highest respect for Bob Taft, not only professionally, but personally. But, some of his people got wind of those letters and they wanted to use them to stop Ike's nomination. Well, I heard about it and I sent Harry Vaughan over to the Pentagon to see if those letters were there—Marshall had since retired. They were, so Vaughan brought them to me, and I sent them to General Marshall, suggesting that he might consider destroying them. He must have done so because that's the last we heard of them. Now that's what I call dirty politics. I certainly never regretted my actions, even though Eisenhower beat our man, Adlai Stevenson, in the election. Hell, he didn't beat him. He buried him! Of course, Adlai buried himself. I'll tell you something, Adlai Stevenson was the original reluctant courtesan. I tried on three separate occasions to get the man to saddle up. I could never get him to commit himself. He always reminded me of the old bird down in Mississippi who was about to die. He called his dear wife to his death bed and said, "Mary, there's a trunk down in the basement that has a bottle of bourbon in it." She said, "I know there is." He said, "Go and fetch it." She did and brought it back. Then he said, "Now, Mary, I want you to get the biggest glass we have in this entire house, and I want you to fill it with ice, put in some

1952 Democratic convention: President Truman with candidate Stevenson

powdered sugar and a little mint, and then I want you to frost it. And Mary, I want you to fill it to the very top with that bourbon, and, no matter what I say, and how much I protest, Mary, make me drink it!" Well, we finally got Stevenson to the trough, but we were never able to make him drink very deeply. I think Stevenson's problem was that he really didn't know how to talk to people. He spent more time trying to figure out how he was going to say something than what he was going to say. He spent a lot more time talking to college presidents than he did to cab drivers, and we've got a hell of a lot more cab drivers in this country than college presidents. Of course, I had my difficulties with Eisenhower. You know, on Ike's inauguration day, I must tell you, I thought Bess and I really were going to have to walk to Union Station just to get a train back home to Missoura. But that's all right, that goes hand in hand with politics. But I'll tell you something that really bothered me about Eisenhower. When he got into the Presidency, he seemed to lose his guts, and it really came home to me when I saw Eisenhower in a picture smiling broadly and shaking hands with a man called William Jenner. Now, that was Senator William Jenner of Indiana. You may remember Jenner as the man who called General Marshall a traitor to his country, and Ike never opened his mouth. Of course, Marshall was the man responsible for Eisenhower's entire career. Eisenhower actually did try one time to defend Marshall.

He rummages through some papers in his portfolio.

President-elect Eisenhower pays a visit

He went up one time to make a speech in Wisconsin. Now, of course, Wisconsin was the stronghold of one *Joseph R. McCarthy.* Well, when Ike arrived in Milwaukee, some of McCarthy's hoods got to him and they convinced Ike that he should delete from his prepared text a defense of General Marshall.

He finds what he's been looking for. He takes the piece of paper in his hand.

Now, these are the words, and I've kept them down through the years. Here they are. These are the words that Ike deleted from his speech that night so as not to offend *Mac the Knife.* He was going to say,

Reading:

"Let me be quite specific. I know that charges of disoloyalty have, in the past, been leveled at General George C. Marshall. I have been privileged for thirty-five years to know General Marshall personally. I know him as a man and a soldier, to be dedicated with singular selflessness and the profoundest patriotism to the service of America. And this episode is a sobering lesson in the way freedom must not defend itself.". . . Now, those are the words he deleted from his speech that night and the subject of the speech was *"freedom."*

He returns the paper to the portfolio.

I have never been able to believe, honestly, that General Eisenhower sacrificed one of the greatest living Americans, in my opinion, to curry the favor of the worst political gangster this country has ever produced, *Joseph McCarthy.* Of course, I attacked that most lamentable mistake of the Almighty every chance I got. I had to. He said that my administration were men and women with lips of traitors. And I tell you folks, if you keep your mouth shut about something like that, democracy simply will not work! Now, I had to take McCarthy on, and I wanted to pick my spot. And, the spot I picked was Massachusetts—Boston, to be exact. For some reason, McCarthy was always very popular in Boston. Even the Democrats up there were very nervous. They wanted me to take it easy on him. Well, when I walked into that Symphony Hall that night, let me tell you, I was prepared to give one hell of a concert! . . .

He walks left to a lectern.

Governor, Mr. Chairman, honored guests. I want to say that it's a pleasure to be back in Boston, and I hope that if I'm ever out of a job that you'll let me come back again sometime. Tonight I'd like to, if I might, deal with some of the fanatics that have enrolled in the so-called great Republican crusade of 1952. Because these fanatics are using a technique developed by one of the worst criminals in the world's history, a man named Adolf Hitler. It's a technique known as the big lie. Now, you all know how that works. You tell a lie so monstrous that it staggers the listener, and then you repeat it over and over again until it's finally accepted as truth. Now, the big lie that these fanatics are telling about my administration is that it is soft on communism. Now, communism is a threat that we all must certainly be aware of, but, my friends, it must never make us lose confidence in *ourselves,* or confidence in *each other,* and most importantly, confidence *in our country.* Because, my friends, it is just as easy, for a Communist, to deceive a Republican, as it is for a Communist to deceive a Democrat. I would like to state that if there are any Communists in my administration, they will be thrown out just as fast as they can be identified. But, my friends, I want to make something else very clear, and that is, that they will not be thrown out without the *due process of law and without sufficient evidence.* Because, by God, I believe in the Bill of Rights of the Constitution of the United States. Now, all of this uproar started when a Republican senator, a denizen of the political underworld, managed to get his hands, we don't know how, but he managed to get his hands on some old security investigations. Now, they were *old* ones. They meant absolutely nothing. But, this senator, *Joseph McCarthy,* dumped them into the public record. Now, as I say, they meant absolutely nothing, and to this day he has not been able to uncover one single Communist, nor will he ever uncover one single Communist, because all he has in that bulging brief case of his is a bottle of booze! And he manages to knock off just about one of those bottles every day. These vicious lies have got to be stopped because every decent citizen in this country who dares to oppose this man of poison tongue is in terrible danger. The reputations of innocent men and women are being butchered at this very moment, and, my friends, that is an *American tragedy! It is tragic! . . .*

> *He puts the text of his speech in his jacket pocket and walks stage center.*

68

You know, I think the best time I ever had in my life was when I took a long train trip across this country in 1948 and talked to just about fifteen million of you people. And I'll be damned if I didn't get my old job back for my trouble. It's a big country. You know it always reminds me of the old cowboy who rode his horse all the way from California to New York City. When he arrived in Times Square, one of those tough Irish cops looked up and said, "Tell me, Hoot Gibson, just how big is this country?" The old boy looked down and he said, "Well, just about as big as your butt can stand to ride it, Buster!" And you know, I really think that was my opponent's problem in '48. Thomas E. Dewey just couldn't stay in the saddle long enough to let all the folks get a look at him. I tried to let as many as I could hear me and look at me. In fact, my train trip became known as the "whistle stop" campaign. Why, we pulled into places in this country that you forget people live. I remember one time we pulled into a place called Dexter, Iowa. Now, you aren't going to believe this, but there were *ninety-six thousand farmers.* It was at about five thirty in the morning, milking time. They were waiting there quietly to hear me talk. Well, really, you know, you don't get ninety-six thousand farmers together at milking time without having an awful lot of nervous cows, and a hell of a run on buttermilk.

He walks to the railroad car.

Sometimes I made as many as fifteen of those speeches in a day, just getting around and talking to *you* people. Now, my opponent, Mr. Dewey, he really didn't talk to people. He talked to the experts, and every one of them said that I was going to lose. I must tell you that it spread some despair and gloom on my campaign train. I remember an assistant of mine, a bright young man and a speech writer named Clark Clifford, coming to me and saying, "Mr. President, I believe you're headed for the gallows." I said, "Clark, listen here, the gallows is just a plaform for the performance of miracle plays in which the central actor is translated to heaven."

He climbs aboard the observation car.

And I was not about to climb those stairs to eternity. So, we kept at it, whistle stopping all the way, and finally we reached the great state of Minnesota. . . . Good morning, folks, it's good to see you, and thank you for turning out so early. This morning I want to pay tribute to the great liberal spirit of this state of Minnesota. And, of course, it's a spirit that derives from a very simple thing in this country, a thing called faith—faith in yourselves, faith in each other, and of course most importantly of all, faith in this great country of ours. And it's a faith, of course, that the Republicans simply cannot understand. Now, you know they won't tell you what they really believe in. Well, by golly, this morning, I'm going to tell you what the Republican party truly believes in, and I can really tell you because I've had a chance to observe that party from very close too, for a long, long time.

He gets wound up.

They tell you, *time and time again.* They say they believe in the American farmer. You bet they do, but they're willing to let him go broke. And they say that they believe in the American home, but not public housing. And they say that they believe in Social Security benefits. It says so right in their platform. All right, the Eightieth Republican Congress just took Social Security benefits away from seven hundred and fifty thousand Americans! Now, they say that they're for a minimum wage. You bet they are, the more *minimumer the better!* And they say that they admire the American way of life, just as long as it doesn't spread to all of the people. And they say that they admire the American government. You bet they do! They admire it so much they want to buy it! Well, we're going to tell them on election day, every one of us, that the American government is *not for sale, now, never, at any price!*

He listens to someone who has called out to him.

No, I'm not giving them hell, mister! No, I just tell the truth on them and that makes them feel like they're in hell! That's right, listen, folks, I'm just running because I want to find a place to live again. You know we got a housing shortage. I don't want to be a burden on the community, that's all. . . . What, ma'm? Do I like speech making? Well, I feel very much like the fella who was on the way to his dear wife's funeral and the funeral director asked him if he'd mind riding in the same car with his mother-in-law to the cemetery, and he said, "I'll do it, but it will ruin my whole day."

He gets a big chuckle.

Yeah, well, that's pretty much the way I feel. . . .
What?

He listens to one of his aides.

Yes, that's right, we've got to get moving, folks. It'll
be about nine more, my goodness, ten more stops
today. Remember, folks, on election day, don't vote
for our party, vote for yourselves, for your interests,
and it'll turn out to be the Democratic party!! Bye,
bye. . . .

*He gets off the platform and walks to a voting
booth. This is old-fashioned, simple type with a
pencil-marking ballot.*

Just before the election, an expert came to see me.
Now, he was a little different kind of an expert. His
name was Leslie Biffle and Les had been the
secretary of the Senate for a number of years, and,
well, he wasn't wired for sound like the Gallups and
the Ropers. He didn't have any machines that he
was attached to. He decked himself out in some old
overalls and rode a spring wagon that was pulled by
two mules, and he posed as a chicken peddler. He
talked to the folks, and when he came back he said,
"Mr. President, you've got nothing to worry about.
The common people are for you." Well, in that
election I did what most people did, I voted the
Democratic ticket right across the board.

72

He steps into the booth, pulls the curtain closed,
marks his ballot, and steps out, beaming. He points
to the election booth.

You know that's the most valuable piece of real
estate in the United States of America, right there. If
we ever sell that, folks, we can just forget about it.
Of course, my opponent in that election did what
most Americans didn't do. He voted for the party
that the experts said would win. And I tell you, after
the election, there was so much crow eaten by the
experts, the conservationists thought that the species
might disappear from the face of the earth.

He picks up a Chicago Tribune.

On our way to Washington, I had a chance to stop in
St. Louis and grab a copy of the *Chicago Tribune—*
the world's greatest newspaper, by its own admission
—and read their banner headline.

He holds the famous pose.

When I got back to Washington, my inauguration
was very opulent, thanks to the Eightieth Republican
Congress, because they thought that their candidate
was going to win and they had appropriated a ton of
money for his inauguration feast. I must say the old
town was so full of liquor that if it could have
walked, it would have staggered!

He goes back into the Oval Office.

You know, most politicians have songs written for them and most of them are pretty bad. I discovered that Thomas E. Dewey had a song written for his inauguration ball. It's a catchy little tune, unfortunately, and he wasn't able to use it. It's a shame he isn't here to perform for you tonight because he has a very fine, rich, church baritone. I'll try to render it for you, in the best sense of that word, but you're going to have to just put up with my quavering Missouri whiskey tenor.

Congratulations, Tom Dewey,
You've won by a landslide today.
Through thick and through thin,
We knew you would win,
'Cause who'd ever vote to let Truman stay in.
Congratulations, Tom Dewey,
Your Republican dreams have come true.
Here's a victory roar—for President
Number thirty-four
The White House is waiting for you.

> *He rises, grabs his cane and Stetson, and heads for the theater aisle.*

Well, let's get out and get some fresh air. I always like to do this every day if I possibly can. Try to keep . . . well, good morning, boys. Nice to see you. How

---

A New York City hike with George Jessel (second from left) and assorted reporters

are you? . . . Well, no, it is nice to see you, I like the press. It's amazing what a man can learn from the newspapers that he didn't know about himself. . . . No, no, listen, I'm just kidding you. I feel about the press the same way Thomas Jefferson did. If I had to chose between no government and no press, I would chose the former every time. . . . Yes, I did, I heard that Nixon called Dean Acheson the "Red Dean." Well, boys, let me tell you something, if Acheson, Marshall, and myself are traitors to this country, we're in one hell of a fix. And I'll tell you something else, Richard Nixon is a no good lying bastard. He can lie out of both sides of his mouth at the same time, and if he ever caught himself telling the truth, he'd lie just to keep his hand in. Now, let's get moving. Out of the way, President of the United States coming through here. We've got to keep going at one-twenty a minute. Say, boys, is there a place around here to strike a blow for liberty? No? Well, remind me not to come this way again. Kennedy? Oh, he's all right. . . . No, no, listen. Kennedy is a good boy—it's his father that bothers me. Well, how many fathers do you know that can buy their sons West Virginia. . . . Now, wait a minute, being Catholic has nothing to do with it. It's not the Pope that worries me, it's the Pop. . . . Where'd I get this cane? It was given to me by the boys in Battery D. When they gave it to me on inauguration day, one of them yelled out, "Don't break it, you clumsy bastard." I've got to watch my language because Nixon is very disturbed about my cussin'. He thinks

Vice-President Richard M. Nixon greets the Ex-President, 1953

the kids are going to copy me and then when they grow up, they'll have to have their mouths washed out with bourbon. There's a story around these days about me, thanks to Nixon. They say, that I'm supposed to say to Margaret when my first grandchild is born, "Margaret, when it gets old enough, I'll teach it how to talk." And she's supposed to say, "The hell you are!"

He stops to talk to a little boy.

What, son? A parade? No, no, this isn't a parade, it's just an old codger trying to keep his blood flowing. . . . Who am I? I'm Harry Truman. Who are you? . . . Tim George, well, Tim, nice to know you. . . . What do I do? Well, I'm President of the United States, Tim. No, I don't run the country. No, sir. A lot of folks are involved in that, Tim. Really what my job is is just to try to keep this country in some sort of working order so that when it comes time to turn it over to you young folks, it'll be in good shape. And I hope you'll do the same when your time comes. It's been going on for over two hundred years now. Well, nice talking to you, Tim. If you ever get to the White House, be sure to look me up. That's where I live. Well, your folks will know where it is. If you get there, you say hello, and I'll be glad to show you around. Bye, Tim.

Harry Truman calls on President John F. Kennedy

78

He crosses back onto the stage.

You know, boys, we've got to keep the youth in this country stirred up. We've got to make them enthused about the history of the country and about the future. The high school kids are fine, but some of the college kids bother me a little bit because when I talk to them—and I do from time to time—they think they know it all. And I always try to tell them that it's what you learn after you know it all that really counts. . . . What do you mean? Eaves what? Eavesdropping. Oh, you mean the bugging of telephones, the listening in on other people's conversation. Well, that's a notorious violation of the Bill of Rights. . . . Super-government? You mean dictatorship. Is that what you are talking about? It will never happen in this country in my opinion. Any guy that tried that would be like the fella that woke up in the coffin with a lily in his hand and said, "If I'm alive, what am I doing here? And, if I'm dead, why do I have to go to the bathroom?" Absolutely, the only way it can happen would be if we had a liar in public office. And I'll tell you, there's nothing more dangerous on this earth than a liar in public office because the people might believe him. And if the folks ever catch him, they should show him just about the amount of compassion that he showed the Constitution. No more, no less! Remember, boys, always do right—it will gratify some, and astonish the rest. You know, boys, this is a great country, built by great people. Do you realize this is the only country in the history of mankind that ever held out a helping hand to all the world, including its enemies. . . . The future? Well, I have

80

no idea. I'm not a prophet. Wait a minute. Now listen. I may be able to give you an answer to that. I've got a poem here that I've carried with me since my high school days. It's Tennyson's "Locksley Hall," and I must have copied it at least twenty times just to keep up on the wear and tear on the paper. You know, this may answer your question about the future. Tennyson said:

For I dipt into the future, far as human eye could see,
Saw the Vision of the World, and all the wonder that would be;
Saw the heavens fill with commerce, argosies of magic sails,
Pilots of the purple twilight, dropping down with costly bales;
Heard the heavens fill with shouting, and there rain'd a ghastly dew
From the nations' airy navies grappling in the central blue;
Far along the world-wide whisper of the south-wind rushing warm,
With the standards of the peoples plunging thro' the thunder-storm;
Till the war-drum throbb'd no longer, and the battle flags were furl'd
In the Parliament of Man, the Federation of the World.
There the common sense of most shall hold a fretful realm in awe,
And the kindly earth shall slumber, lapt in universal law.

He looks around. He is alone.

81

They're gone. Well, at least I know how to get rid of
the press.

It amuses him.

I'm glad because that leaves just you and me now,
and I've got to leave this office, this job, this honor
that you bestowed on me. You know, one of our
founding fathers, Benjamin Franklin, dealt with this
very moment. He said, "In a free society, the rulers
are the servants, and the people are their superiors
and sovereigns. For the former, therefore, to return
to the latter is not to degrade them, but to promote
them." My promotion is to be one of you.

He exits.

Harry S. Truman, private citizen